IF I MET AN ICE AGE ANIMAL

IF I DINED WITH DIRE WOLVES

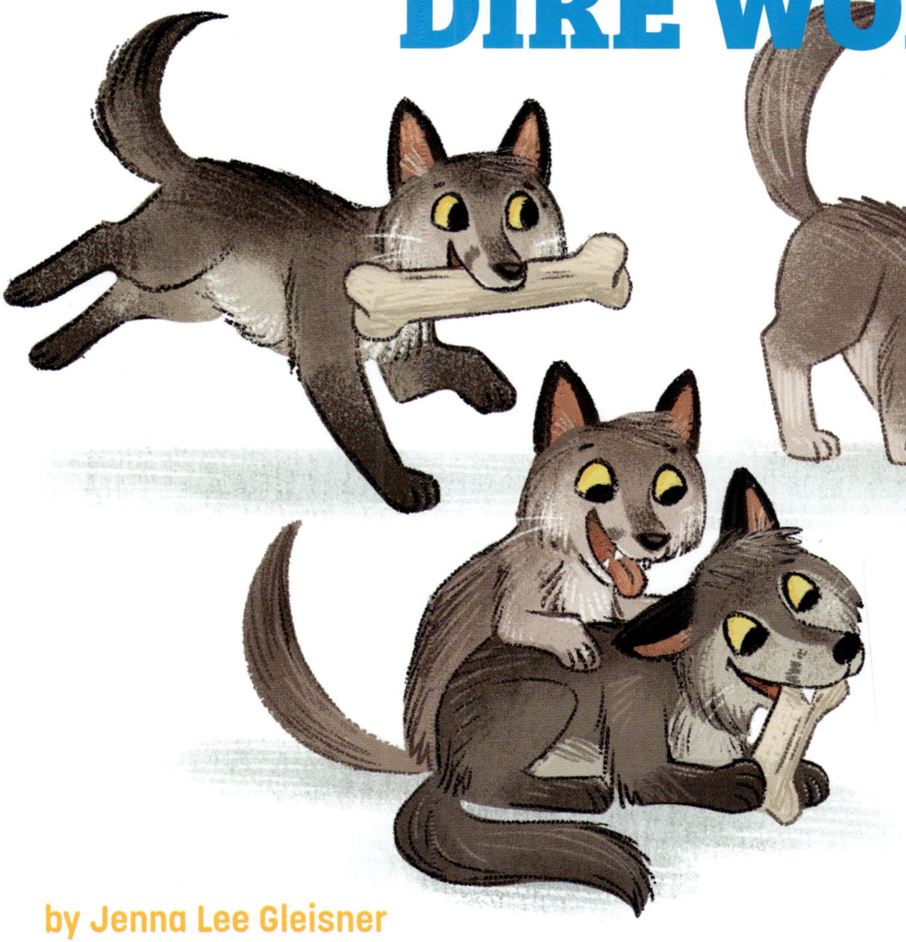

by Jenna Lee Gleisner

illustrated by Michelle Simpson

I0806886

GRASSHOPPER

Tools for Parents & Teachers

Grasshopper Books enhance imagination and introduce the earliest readers to fiction with fun storylines and illustrations. The easy-to-read text supports early reading experiences with repetitive sentence patterns and sight words.

Before Reading

- Discuss the cover illustration. What do readers see?
- Look at the picture glossary together. Discuss the words.

Read the Book

- Read the book to the child, or have him or her read independently.
- "Walk" through the book and look at the illustrations. Who is the main character? What is happening in the story?

After Reading

- Prompt the child to think more. Ask: The main character imagines hunting with a pack of dire wolves. If you could spend a day with a group of animals, what group would it be? What would you do with them?

Grasshopper Books are published by Jump!
5357 Penn Avenue South
Minneapolis, MN 55419
www.jumplibrary.com

Copyright © 2023 Jump! International copyright reserved in all countries. No part of this book may be reproduced in any form without written permission from the publisher.

Library of Congress Cataloging-in-Publication Data

Names: Gleisner, Jenna Lee, author.
Simpson, Michelle, illustrator.
Title: If I dined with dire wolves / by Jenna Lee Gleisner;
illustrated by Michelle Simpson.
Description: Minneapolis, MN: Jump!, Inc., 2023.
Series: If I met an Ice Age animal | Includes index.
Audience: Ages 5-8.
Identifiers: LCCN 2021060744 (print)
LCCN 2021060745 (ebook)
ISBN 9781636909394 (hardcover)
ISBN 9781636909400 (paperback)
ISBN 9781636909417 (ebook)
Subjects: CYAC: Dire wolf–Fiction. | Wolves–Fiction.
Prehistoric animals–Fiction. | LCGFT: Picture books.
Classification: LCC PZ7.1.G5885 If 2023 (print)
LCC PZ7.1.G5885 (ebook)
DDC [E]–dc23
LC record available at https://lccn.loc.gov/2021060744
LC ebook record available at https://lccn.loc.gov/2021060745

Editor: Eliza Leahy
Direction and Layout: Anna Peterson
Illustrator: Michelle Simpson

Printed in the United States of America at
Corporate Graphics in North Mankato, Minnesota.

Table of Contents

Part of the Pack

"Mom, we learned about dire wolves today!" my twin brother says.

"Would they have eaten soup for dinner, too?" she asks.

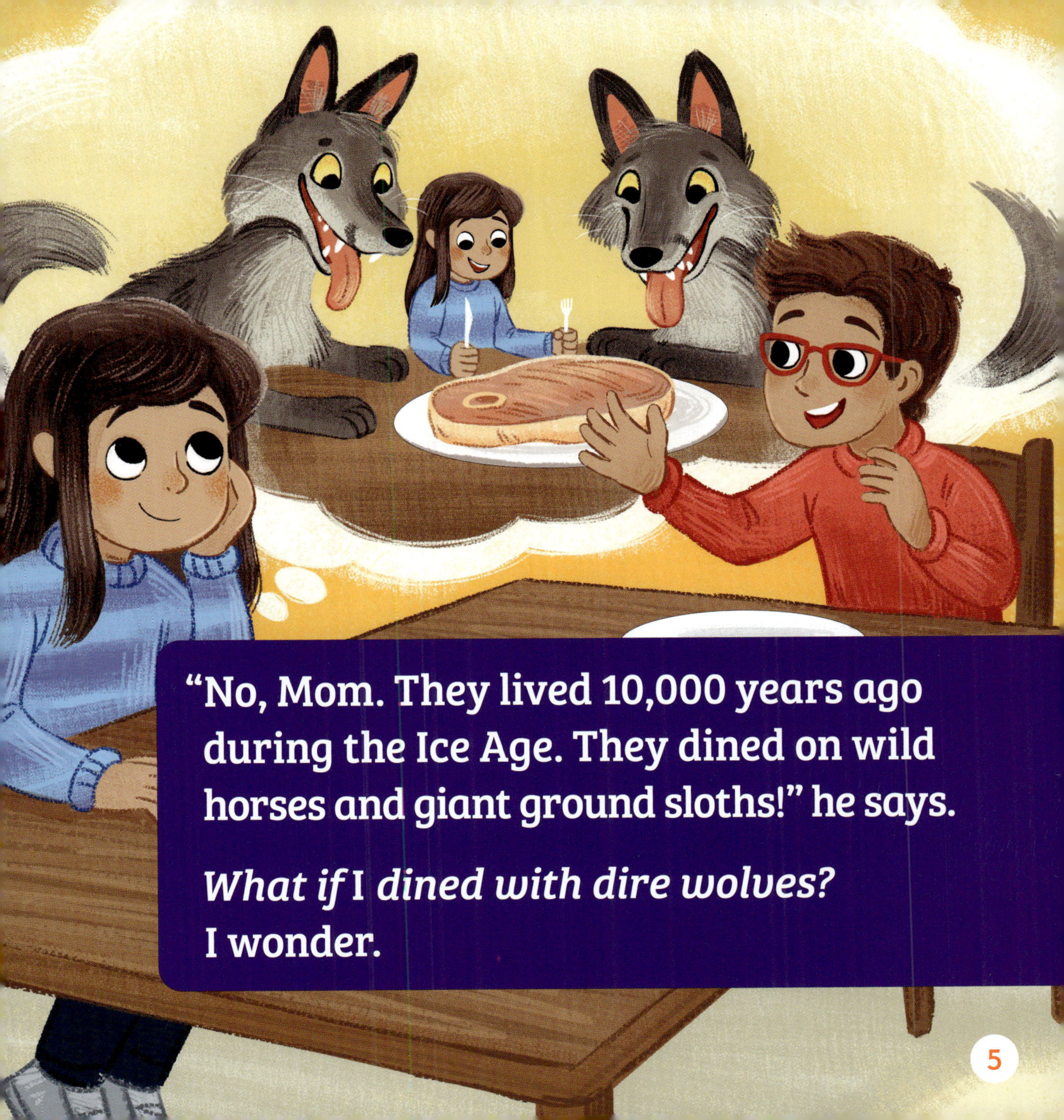

"No, Mom. They lived 10,000 years ago during the Ice Age. They dined on wild horses and giant ground sloths!" he says.

What if I *dined with dire wolves?* I wonder.

If I dined with dire wolves,
I would bundle up.

During the Ice Age,
everything was covered
in ice and snow. *Brr!*

Dire wolves had thick
fur to keep them warm.

We would hunt! Dire wolves were carnivores. They lived and hunted in packs. A pack could have up to 30 wolves.

If I hunted with dire wolves, I would hear them howl.

Awoooooo!

One of the wolves found dinner!

We would run to him. Dire wolves were fast and strong. I'd run fast to keep up.

The pack found a giant ground sloth to eat. If I hunted with dire wolves, I might see a short-faced bear. These bears hunted giant ground sloths, too. But hunting in a pack helps the wolves.

Dinnertime!

short-faced bear
giant ground sloth

After the hunt, I would follow the pack to its den.

den

The wolves would cut the food with their big, strong teeth. Then they would share it with me.

"No, thank you!" I'd say. "My mom is making food at home!"

Even the pups would get some.

If I dined with dire wolves, we would nap after. Some wolves would chew on the bones.

Slurp!

Then I hear another slurp.

“Yum!” says my brother.
“Why aren’t you eating?”

“I was imagining dining
with dire wolves,” I say.

“You can’t. They’re extinct!”
he says.

Parts of a Dire Wolf

Dire wolves weighed up to 175 pounds (79 kilograms). They were about six feet (1.8 meters) long from snout to tail. Take a look at the parts of a dire wolf.

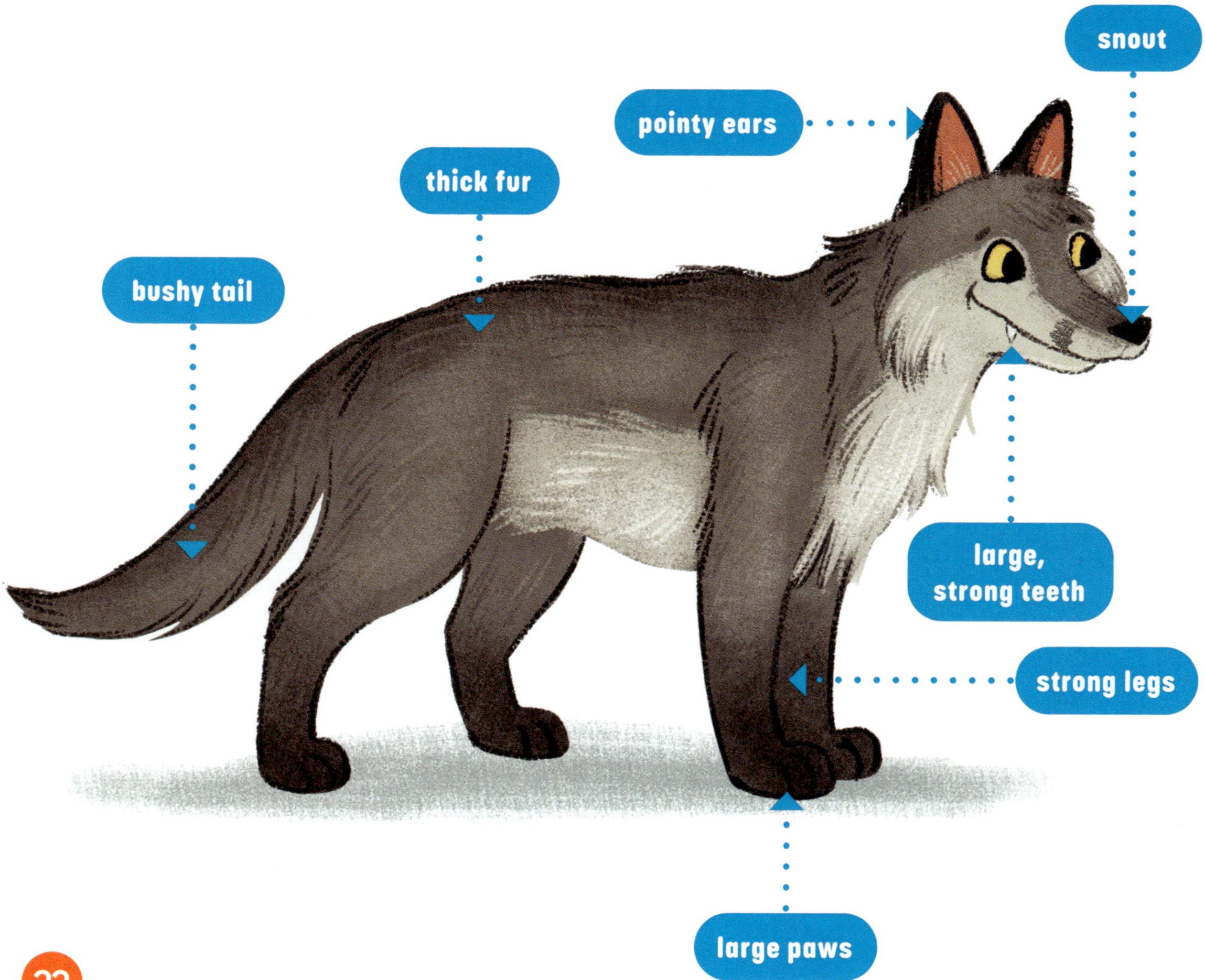

Picture Glossary

carnivores
Animals that eat meat.

extinct
No longer found alive and known about only through fossils or history.

howl
To make a long, loud cry.

Ice Age
A period of time, about 10,000 years ago, when a large part of Earth was covered with ice.

packs
Groups of dire wolves.

pups
Baby dire wolves.

Index

To Learn More

FACT SURFER

Finding more information is as easy as 1, 2, 3.

1. Go to www.factsurfer.com
2. Enter "**ifIdinedwithdirewolves**" into the search box.
3. Choose your book to see a list of websites.